D0384926

THE USBORNE BOOK OF
BEADS, BANGLES AND BRACELETS

Ray Gibson

Edited by Nicole Irving · Designed by Vicki Groombridge
Illustrated by John Woodcock · Photographs by Howard Allman
Series editor: Cheryl Evans

With thanks to Elaine Miller and Kate Foyster

Contents

Getting started

This book shows you how to make lovely bracelets and lots of wonderful beads, which you can use to make original things to wear. Always read through each project before you begin. Below are some tips and simple techniques that will help you.

Threading beads

Thread beads onto a needle with a double thread.

Tape the end to hold the beads. Once you have threaded the beads on, finish with a double knot.

Here are some other ideas for threading beads. You can buy these things from craft suppliers or places that sell thread.

Fine elastic: thread it onto a needle with a big eye, or just push the elastic through beads. See right for how much to use.

Leather thong: to hang a pendant, fold the thong in half. Push both ends through the hole from the back. Pull them almost all the way through then slip them through the loop in the thong. Pull them tight and tie the ends.

A thong or lace can also be pushed through big beads, or try gift tie, string, embroidery threads, or ribbon.

Threading tiny beads

Use thread or fishing line, also called nylon thread. This is strong and invisible, and you can just push it through beads.

Measuring a bracelet or necklace

To make sure it fits, hold the ends together, try passing it over your head or hand, then add about 5cm (2in) for knotting the ends together. With elastic, measure what you need without stretching it (a tight fit will work, though, as the elastic will stretch).

To make something for an adult, allow extra length.

Making a bead stand

A stand stops beads from rolling around, and is useful for other reasons too (see right).

1. Cut four layers of newspaper into a long strip 12cm (5in) wide. Fold the strip in two, bringing the long sides together.

2. Fold each half down to meet the middle fold. Place this stand on a tray if you think you will want to move it around.

Place the beads in the middle gulley.

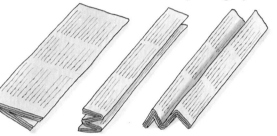

Using a bead stand

Use a stand to calculate how many beads you need. Measure how long you want the necklace or bracelet (see left), make a stand that is longer and mark the length you are working toward on it. Fill the stand until you reach the mark: you now have enough beads.

A stand also makes it easy to thread beads in size or pattern order (see page 14).

Lay beads on the stand in the order in which you want them. Working from one end of the stand to the other, push your threaded needle through each bead. Tie the two thread ends together in a double knot.

Buying beads

Beads are expensive to buy. When you make your own, though, think of mixing them with beads from a broken necklace or just a few beads from a craft supplier.

Tiny glass beads do not cost very much and look good with handmade beads. They can also decorate bigger things that you make.

Tiny glass beads come in lots of shapes and sizes.

Long glass beads

Look out for jars or boxes of mixed glass beads.

Things you can buy

Here are a few things you may want to buy from a craft supplier. For how to use them, see page 32.

Brooch backs

A safety pin is often all you need for the back of a brooch. Just sew it on.

Earring attachments

For unpierced ears

For pierced ears

3

Rolled paper beads

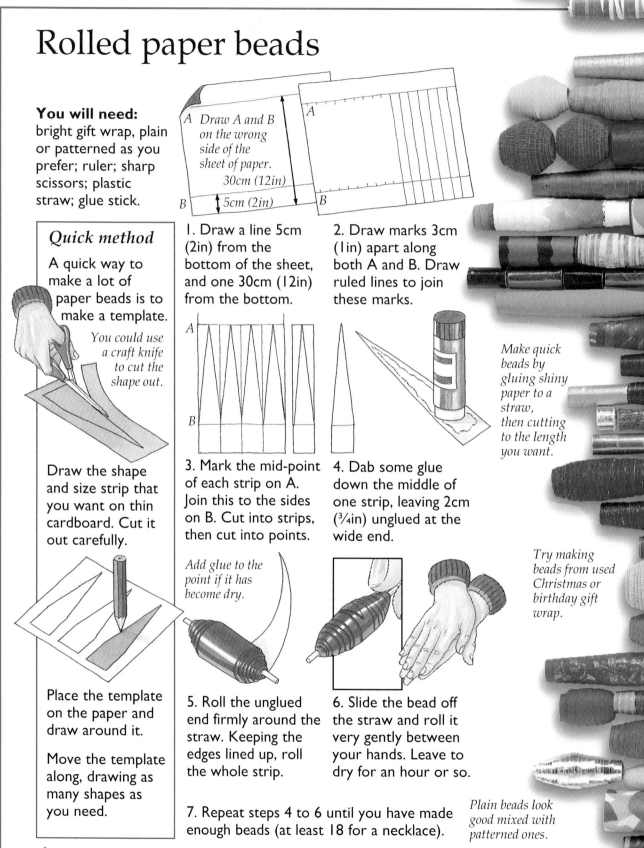

You will need:
bright gift wrap, plain or patterned as you prefer; ruler; sharp scissors; plastic straw; glue stick.

A Draw A and B on the wrong side of the sheet of paper.
30cm (12in)
5cm (2in)

Quick method

A quick way to make a lot of paper beads is to make a template.

You could use a craft knife to cut the shape out.

Draw the shape and size strip that you want on thin cardboard. Cut it out carefully.

Place the template on the paper and draw around it.

Move the template along, drawing as many shapes as you need.

1. Draw a line 5cm (2in) from the bottom of the sheet, and one 30cm (12in) from the bottom.

2. Draw marks 3cm (1in) apart along both A and B. Draw ruled lines to join these marks.

3. Mark the mid-point of each strip on A. Join this to the sides on B. Cut into strips, then cut into points.

Add glue to the point if it has become dry.

4. Dab some glue down the middle of one strip, leaving 2cm (¾in) unglued at the wide end.

5. Roll the unglued end firmly around the straw. Keeping the edges lined up, roll the whole strip.

6. Slide the bead off the straw and roll it very gently between your hands. Leave to dry for an hour or so.

7. Repeat steps 4 to 6 until you have made enough beads (at least 18 for a necklace).

Make quick beads by gluing shiny paper to a straw, then cutting to the length you want.

Try making beads from used Christmas or birthday gift wrap.

Plain beads look good mixed with patterned ones.

Paper beads are strong, light and cheap to make. They also look good mixed with other beads.

More paper beads

Long beads: make beads as in steps 1-7, but wider; in step 2, draw marks 4 or 5cm apart (1 or 1½in).

Fat beads: use thick paper for these fat beads. Follow steps 1-7, but in step 1, draw line A 50cm (20in) from the bottom; in step 2, draw marks 1½cm (½in) apart.

Newspaper beads: make long beads from newspaper. Paint them using acrylic paints.

Thick crêpe makes good beads.

Cylinder beads: cut straight strips of paper 2½ x 30cm (1 x 12in) and follow steps 4-7 opposite.

Small gold beads: using gold paper, draw and cut out straight strips of 1½ x 20cm (½ x 8in). Follow steps 4-7, but roll around a toothpick instead of a straw.

Tiny silver beads: using silver paper, cut straight strips ½ x 20cm (¼ x 8in). Roll around a toothpick.

Varnishing

Varnishing paper beads helps to strengthen them. Use household glue (PVA) mixed with a little water. This glue will dry perfectly clear. Thread single beads on toothpicks. Stick these in half a clean, dry potato. Carefully paint the varnish on from top to bottom, then leave to dry.

5

Clay pigs and apples

You will need: pink, green and red oven-hardening clay; silver florists' wire; baking tray; kitchen foil; three toothpicks; clear tape; craft knife; old scissors; fine elastic; large needle.
For a necklace: make 4 pigs and about 40 apple beads.
For a bracelet: 3 pigs, 15 apples.

Pig beads

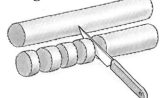

1. Soften a little pink clay in your hands. Roll it into a sausage shape and cut this into pea-sized pieces. Roll one into a ball.

Tip

To make all your beads the same size, roll some clay into a sausage shape. Cut this in half and keep cutting each piece in half until you reach the right size.

How to make wire loops

For each pig bead you need a loop made like this:

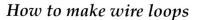

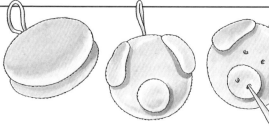

Twist the toothpicks.

Slip the loop off. Trim to 1½cm (¾in).

1. Tape together two toothpicks. Loop a piece of wire about 9cm (4in) long around them.

2. Bring the wire together under the sticks and hold it firmly. Keep holding it during step 3.

3. Twist the sticks around three or four times. The wire winds around itself, leaving a loop.

The loop must be at this angle.

2. Cover the upturned baking tray with foil. Put the clay ball near its edge, press it and put a wire loop (see above) in the middle.

3. Flatten another ball a little more than the first, to make it larger. Press it over the first, covering the wire stem.

4. Roll two small pear shapes for ears and press them on. Add a small round snout. Mark eyes and nostrils with a toothpick.

Apple beads

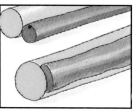

1. Soften some green clay and roll it into a sausage shape. Add a fine strip of softened red clay to the side. Gently roll together.

2. For each bead, cut a pea-sized piece and roll it into a ball (see Tip). Put it on the upturned tray. Pierce with a toothpick.

Baking and threading

Bake at gas mark1/ 140°C/275°F for 10 to 15 minutes, or follow what the packet says. Ask an adult to help.

Once the clay is cold, thread the beads on enough elastic for a bracelet or a necklace (see page 2). Tie with a double knot.

Try mixing shades of clay for a marbled effect. This bracelet mixes 10 marbled beads and 20 plain ones, threaded on elastic. For more on making marbled beads, see the next page.

Put four apple beads between each pig.

Make a variety of plain, bright beads to thread together. Follow the Tip to get them all one size.

For a fruit necklace, make 5 bananas, 30 oranges, 5 strawberries and 30 apples.

Fruit cocktail

What you need: as for pigs and apples, but green, red, yellow, orange and black clay; sandpaper.

Banana: roll a thin yellow sausage with a strip of black, 5cm (2in) long. Slice it in two. Put a piece on the upturned tray. Lay a wire loop on it. Put the other piece on top. Press them gently together, pick them up and shape into a banana.

Strawberry: shape a ball of red clay into a strawberry shape. Cut a leaf from a slice of green clay. Put this on the shape and push a loop in. Mark seeds with a toothpick.

Orange: roll a pea-sized ball of orange clay on the sandpaper. Put it on the foil and pierce it with a toothpick.

Marbled beads

What you need: three shades of oven-hardening clay; baking tray; kitchen foil; toothpick; craft knife.

Press gently.

1. Soften the clay. Roll three sausage shapes of equal length. Place them together and press them.

2. Pick them up and roll them in between the palms of your hands until they form a single shape.

The more you do this, the more the shades mix.

3. Cut this roll into three pieces of equal length. Repeat steps 1-3 until the roll has lots of stripes.

4. Cut into pea-sized pieces (see Tip, page 6). Roll each one into a ball and finish as for Apple beads, page 6.

Streaky bracelet

What you need: as above; also, darning needle; fine elastic.

1. Follow steps 1-3 above. Cut the striped roll into thin slices. As you do this, the base flattens a little.

2. Lay the slices on the foil covered baking tray. Pierce two holes with the needle. Bake and cool (see page 6).

The holes must let a darning needle through.

3. Keeping the beads' flat bases together, thread elastic through one side, then back through the other.

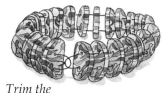

Trim the ends of the elastic.

4. To finish, thread one of the elastic ends through the loop, and knot it with the other loose end.

Make about 40 beads for a bracelet.

For the brown necklace, make thin slices from a narrow sausage of marbled clay. Pierce them with a single hole.

8

Plant beads

To make these beads, use dry, hollow stems from the garden, or you could buy some dried flowers. Many flower stems give good results, for example: roses, foxgloves, large poppies, delphiniums.

String painted and plain plant beads onto double thread with glass beads.

Dry poppy heads look good with these beads. Carefully push the needle through their base.

What you need: dried stems; scissors; craft knife; needle; thread; toothpick.

A few pieces of stem may crack while you are cutting. Throw them away.

How to cut thick stems

Saw gently without trying to cut through completely.

1. Saw around the stem, just enough to mark a line on it.

Trim away any jagged edges using scissors.

2. You can now neatly snap the stem.

Decorate with a gold or silver felt-tip pen, leaving some of the stem bare.

1. Snip off any weak or broken parts of the stems, and any rough growth.

2. Cut thin stems to the length you want. For thick stems, see the box above.

3. Before threading, push a toothpick gently through thicker stems.

Friendship bracelets

Friendship bracelets may seem hard to make when you first try. Don't give up, though, as you soon get the hang of the technique. Then you can experiment with patterns to make completely individual bracelets for a particular friend.

What you need: three shades of six-stranded embroidery thread; clear tape; scissors.

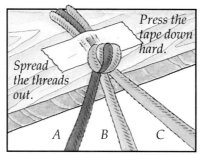

1. Cut a 70cm (28in) long piece of each shade of thread. Knot these together 6cm (2½in) from one end. Tape this end firmly to a table edge.

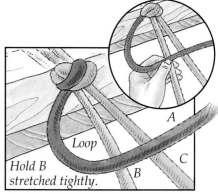

2. Hold thread B with your left hand.* Bring thread A over B with your right hand, leaving a loop. Hold it with your left thumb along with B.

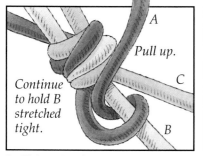

3. Take the free end of A under B, then up through the loop, making a loose knot. Slide the knot up to the top, pulling A firmly to tighten it.

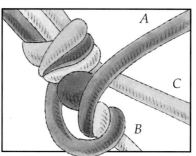

4. Repeat step 3, taking A around B once again, then up through the loop into a loose knot. Pull A to tighten. You now have two knots.

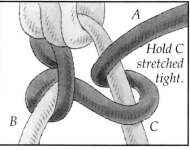

5. Let go of thread B, and take hold of C instead. Knot A onto C twice in the same way. A is now on the right, and you have made the first row.

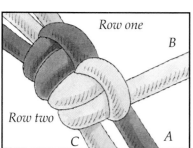

6. Start row two, knotting from left to right: knot B twice onto C, then twice onto A. For row 3, knot C twice onto A, then onto B.

7. Keep making new rows from left to right until you have enough length to go around your wrist. Tie the three loose ends in a knot.

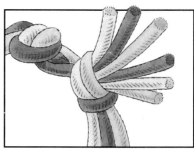

8. Put the bracelet around a friend's wrist, make a double knot, then trim all the ends. To tie it to your own wrist, ask a friend to do it for you.

10

*Change hands around if you are left-handed.

Sizes and patterns

For a wider bracelet, tie four, five or six threads together and knot each thread twice from left to right in the usual way. Create patterns by using several threads of the same shade, then one or more of another shade.

Each thread gives a row. The shades repeat in the same order.

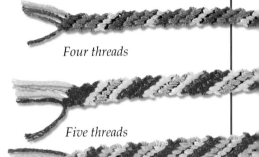

Four threads

Five threads

Six threads

Safety pin method

Try wearing three or more friendship bracelets together. They look especially good when you wear them like this.

Instead of taping the threads to a table (step 1), push a safety pin through the knot in the threads. Sit down and push the pin into your jeans just above your knee.

Beaded bracelets

Push a thread that you are about to start knotting through a bead, then knot twice in the usual way.

Use the different shades of thread as a guide to space the beads evenly.

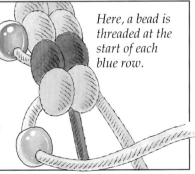

Here, a bead is threaded at the start of each blue row.

Metal heart pendants

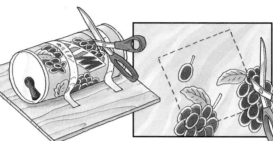

What you need:
clean, empty soft drink can; clear tape; old gloves; rag; old scissors; pencil; small hammer; glue stick; 6 x 6cm (2½ x 2½in) piece of tracing paper; pencil; sandpaper; flat piece of wood; nail; two small pieces of cardboard.

1. Tape the can firmly to a flat surface. Ask an adult to pierce a hole with the scissors. Remove the tape.

2. Put on the gloves. Push the scissors into the hole. Cut a square about 6 x 6cm (2½in x 2½in).

3. Flatten the metal square by bending it back, and then rubbing it firmly with the rag on a flat surface.

Trim the trace to the size of the square.

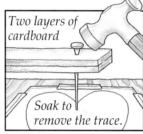

Two layers of cardboard

Soak to remove the trace.

4. Trace the big heart template, with a mark for the hole. Glue the trace to the metal square's plain side.

5. Tape the square to the piece of wood. Use the nail to press a dent in where the hole mark is.

6. Push the nail through the cardboard. Hold this and place the nail in the dent. Tap the nail through the metal.

7. Cut out the heart. Use sandpaper to smooth the edges and around the hole on the other side.

For a brooch, take a thread through a bow, a bead, a pendant, and back the same way. See page 3 to finish.

Jewel heart

Follow steps 1-7 to make a big heart, plain side up (put the trace on the patterned side). **You also need:** kitchen foil; bright foil wrapper.

Flatten the bottom of the jewel.

Use lots of glue and leave to dry.

1. Crumple some foil. Wrap it in the bright wrapper. Press this jewel on a flat surface.

2. Glue the jewel to the middle of the heart. Glue a strip of folded foil around it.

Embossed pendant

What you need: flat piece of metal (see steps 1-3 left); fine felt-tip pen; old ball-point pen; paper towels; hole-punch; leather thong.

For this effect, paint the pendant with acrylic paint. See page 2 to find out how to hang a pendant on a leather thong.

Allow room for the hole.

Check the hole will be where you want before punching.

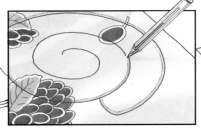

1. Place the metal, pattern side up, on a pad of paper towels. Draw a design with the felt-tip pen.

2. Go over the design firmly with the ball-point pen enough times to make raised lines on the other side.

3. Cut around the shape, just outside the outer raised edge. Punch a hole for the thong, then sand the edges.

Heart template

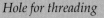

Hole for threading

For the felt heart on page 18, trace the big template.

The small shape is good for the velvet choker. You could also use it for a brooch.

Velvet choker

What you need: small plain heart pendant; acrylic paint; fine paintbrush; 37cm (14½in) velvet ribbon, 1½cm (½in) wide; silver paper bead (page 4); a few tiny glass beads and sequins; needle; thread; Velcro.

Put a knot in the end of the thread.

1. Paint the middle of the heart. Once dry, scratch on a pattern.

2. Find the middle of the ribbon. Sew a double thread through an edge.

Decorate with beads and sequins.

Finish with tiny stitches.

3. Thread through the paper bead and the heart, and back the same way to the ribbon.

4. Fold over the ends of the ribbon. Sew 2cm (¾in) Velcro to each end.

Big bold beads

For a necklace you need:
a newspaper bead stand (see pages 2-3), on a tray; kitchen foil; ruler; scissors; old gloves; papier mâché pulp (see box); large needle (for tapestry or darning); fine elastic; acrylic paints; paintbrush.

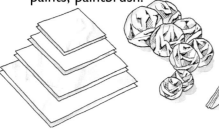

1. For a large, central bead, cut a square of foil 20 x 20cm (8 x 8in). Crumple and press this into a ball.

Make the foil ball as round as possible.

2. Put on the gloves. Roll the ball firmly between the palms of your hands. Place it in the middle of the bead stand.

3. Make two smaller foil balls from 18cm (7in) squares, then two each from 16, 14 and 12cm squares (6, 5 and 4in).

4. Put the foil balls on the stand, placing one of each size on either side so they are in size order, from big to small.

The pulp must cover all the foil.

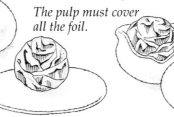

The different patterns on these beads look good together because they are all painted on using the same shades of paint.

Biggest bead in the middle.

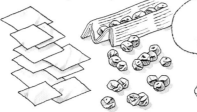

5. Make foil balls from 10cm (3in) squares to add to both ends to make the length you need for a necklace.

6. For each foil ball, roll a ball of pulp of about the same size. Flatten this into a circle and wrap it around the foil ball.

The beads shrink a little as they dry.

A coat of white paint is a good base for decorating.

7. Roll the ball gently between your palms to make it round and smooth. Put it back on the stand. Cover all the foil balls.

8. Leave the beads to dry on the stand in a warm place. Occasionally, roll each bead gently and put back to dry.

9. Once dry, pierce a hole through each one using the needle. Paint white all over, dry, then decorate by painting.

Quick foil beads

Make beads as in steps 1-5. Don't add any papier mâché pulp; just pierce a hole straight into the foil. To decorate, put a little paint in your palms and roll the foil beads between them. Leave to dry. If you like, you can roll them a second time with another shade of paint.

The beads below are made from foil only. They are rolled in a little paint so that the silver shows through. For a very sophisticated look, you could roll foil beads in black paint and thread them with tiny black glass beads.

Papier mâché pulp

What you need: scissors; newspaper; bowl; mug; hot water; household glue (PVA); tablespoon; mesh sieve; blender (if you like).

1. Cut some layers of newspaper to make 1½cm (½in) squares (enough to half fill the mug when lightly pressed).

2. Soak this paper for three hours in hot water, then squeeze and mash it with your fingers to turn it into pulp (or mush).

3. Another way to make pulp is to put the dry paper squares in a blender, cover with water and blend in short bursts.

Ask permission before using the blender.

4. Pour into a mesh sieve and press out most of the water. Tip the pulp into a bowl. Use your fingers to mix in a tablespoon of glue.

5. Keep mixing and adding a little glue until the pulp feels like squishy clay.

You can store the pulp in a jar in a refrigerator if you like. Mix before using.

This is enough for the beads you make on page 14.

Paper fans

For a necklace, you need: sheet of ½cm (¼in) graph paper; scissors; hard pencil; ruler; gold or silver pen (if wanted); felt-tip pens; long double thread on a needle; beads for step 10 (ready-made or paper beads - see page 4); matt polyurethane varnish; small paint brush.

This is the right side of the paper.

1. Draw a rectangle 19 x 3½cm (7½ x 1¼in) on the graph paper. Cut it out very carefully.

2. Follow the lines on the paper to score a line every 1cm (½in) (scoring is drawing while pressing hard).

3. Turn the paper over. Score a line ½cm (¼in) from the left edge, then every 1cm (½in) to the end.

4. Use felt-tips to fill the squares, making a regular pattern. Now varnish over this if you like (see right).

5. Add gold or silver checks or triangles, or a scribbled pattern over other shades. Let it dry thoroughly.

6. Turn the paper over. Fold down ½cm (¼in), along the scored line. Then fold back, ½cm (¼in) along.

7. Continue until all the paper is carefully folded. Gently squeeze to sharpen the folds.

Paper fans make lovely earrings. Use nylon thread (fishing wire - see page 2) in step 8, pass both ends through a bead or two, then tie with a double knot to an earring attachment (see page 3).

Card beads look good threaded with paper beads (page 3).

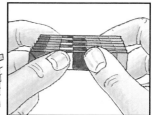

Middle of the top square

8. Push the needle through the first two folds, top right, then through the other folds, two at a time.

9. Draw the thread through so the fan is in the middle. Gather the folds, then tie the thread at the top.

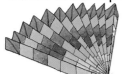

Using beads 1cm (¾ in) wide, you need about 46.

10. Take the ends of the threads up through a bead. Separate in two and add beads to each.

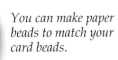

You can make paper beads to match your card beads.

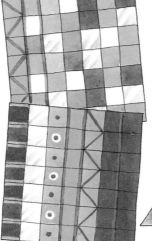

Fan patterns

Design your own fan or copy one of these. You can do solid bands on the top, as checks will not show.

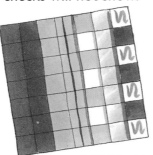

Varnishing

After step 4, paint on a thin coat of varnish. Stand the fan in a warm place to dry before going on to step 5. You can also varnish card beads.

Recycled card beads

For a bead, you need: wire-loop (as shown on page 6, but loop the wire around one toothpick and leave a long tail); small bead; greetings card; pencil; scissors; small round jar; glue stick; darning needle; clear tape.

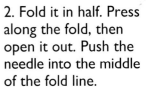

Wiggle the needle around to make the hole big enough for the wire loop.

1. Choose a part of the card that you like. Place the jar on it, draw around it and cut out the circle.

2. Fold it in half. Press along the fold, then open it out. Push the needle into the middle of the fold line.

Trim the tail if it is too long.

The photographs below show how the wire loops are twisted.

3. Thread the loop through the bead, then through the hole in the circle. Tape the tail down.

4. Glue the two sides together. Leave to dry. Twist the loop, so that it will lie correctly when threaded.

For small card beads, start with a half-circle. Fold in two, tape a wire loop inside, then glue the two sides together.

Felt beads

For a felt heart, you need: felt squares; tracing paper; pencil; pins; sharp scissors; needle and thread; padding such as knitting yarn cut into small pieces; glass or paper bead (see page 4); a few tiny beads and sequins.

1. Trace the big heart shape on page 13. Pin this trace on a double layer of felt (different shades if you like). Cut out the shape.

2. Take off the trace. Pin the hearts together. Tack* around the edges, leaving a gap big enough for a finger.

3. Take out the pins. Sew tiny running stitches neatly around the edge with double thread, leaving the gap open.

4. Take out the tacks. Stuff the heart tightly with the padding. Sew up the gap. Finish by stitching a few times in the same place.

5. Sew a double thread through the middle of the heart, at the top. Then sew up through a glass or paper bead.

Sew on a few sequins or tiny beads.

For a simple pendant that looks good on a T-shirt, hang a padded heart on a thong. Attach it by taking the thread around the thong a few times, then back into the heart. Finish with a few tiny stitches.

Rolled felt bead

What you need: felt square; pins; graph paper; toothpick; glue stick; pencil; ruler; scissors.

1. Draw a strip 1cm (½in) wide on the graph paper. Cut it out, then pin it to the felt and cut along its edge.

2. Take off the paper. Roll the felt strip tightly around the toothpick until the bead is the size you want. Trim the end.

3. Holding the felt firmly, gently pull the toothpick out. Glue the loose end down securely and leave to dry.

Stripy rolls

Make rolled beads from two strips of felt in contrasting shades. Roll them together around a toothpick. Glue the inner loose end down, then the outer one.

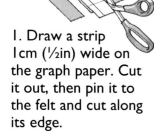

18

Tacking is when you sew big, loose stitches which you will later remove.

For the necklace above, thread rolled felt beads on fine elastic. To make beads with a staggered effect, roll a strip of felt, glue, then roll another shade and glue.

Bound felt beads

What you need: felt squares; plastic straws; glue stick; embroidery threads; knitting yarns; gold or silver thread; tiny glass beads; scissors.

Slip a few glass beads on the threads.

1. Glue one side of a strip of felt and wrap around a straw. Trim the straw at each end.

2. Bind each bead with yarn and threads. Tie these securely. Trim the ends neatly.

For a necklace, thread eight beads on a few strands of embroidery thread. For a bracelet, thread six beads on enough fine elastic to go over your hand (see page 2).

Make a padded fish bead (use the large template on page 23 if you like), and attach it to a thong like the heart on the left.

Felt bead necklace

You need: a heart; one big and four smaller rolled beads; 70cm (28in) double thread on a thin needle; glass beads; masking tape.

1. Stitch the heart to the big bead. Thread glass beads to fill 26cm (10in) of the double thread.

Tape to hold the beads.

2. Then push the needle through two smaller beads, the big one, and the other two smaller ones. Cover the remaining thread with glass beads and knot the thread ends together.

Jungle bangles

You need: papier mâché pulp (see page 15; make half the amount); scissors; thin cardboard; ruler; clear tape; craft knife; pencil; household glue (PVA); newspaper; empty jar; plastic foodwrap; acrylic paints.

Trim here.

1. Cut a 2½cm (1in) wide cardboard strip. Bend it into a circle that passes over your wrist. Cut it to size.

2. Tape this circle around a jar that is about the same size. Add extra tape so it does not slip down.

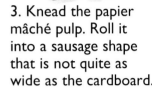

3. Knead the papier mâché pulp. Roll it into a sausage shape that is not quite as wide as the cardboard.

4. Hold the jar on its side. Press one end of the pulp onto the cardboard. Press the rest around the jar.

5. Break off the pulp shape where the ends join and smooth these together, pressing lightly.

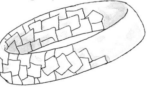

6. Gently push the pulp to the edges of the cardboard strip. Make an even, rounded shape.

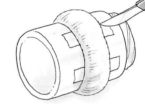

7. Leave to dry for at least a day in a warm, airy place. Then slit the tape holding the bangle and slide off.

8. Tear newspaper into 1½cm (½in) squares. Mix together equal amounts of glue and water.

9. Dip the squares in the mixture and cover both sides of the bangle with them. Overlap them.

10. Cover with four layers for a smooth finish. Leave to dry on some foodwrap, turning occasionally.

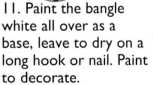

Now varnish.

11. Paint the bangle white all over as a base, leave to dry on a long hook or nail. Paint to decorate.

Decorating bangles

Here are some ideas for decorating old bangles. You could also buy bangles that don't cost much and decorate them.

Painting a wooden bangle:
rub all over with fine sandpaper, then paint and varnish (see steps 10-11).

Painting a plastic bangle:
stick on two layers of torn paper (see steps 8-9). Paint and varnish following steps 10-11.

Découpage bangle:
découpage is a French word that means cutting out. Paint a bangle all over. Cut out small shapes like flowers or leaves from bright gift wrap. Glue them on the bangle, then add three coats of varnish (see box).

Glitzy bangle:
take any bangle. Dab paint on a piece of foil. Leave to dry, then cut the foil into 1½cm (¾in) strips. Glue one end of a strip on the bangle, wind it around. Glue the other end. Keep winding strips around, overlapping them a little, until the bangle is covered. Neatly cover with short pieces of clear tape, then smooth by polishing with a soft cloth.

Varnishing

Mix two tablespoons of glue with one of water. Use a paint brush to varnish the bangle with this. Once dry, varnish once more.

The glue and water mixture is white, but it dries clear.

Leaves and fish

Remove the top and the bottom to make a plastic tube.

For a fish bead you need: large, clear plastic soft drink bottle; pencil; craft knife; scissors; waterproof felt-tip pen; plastic straw; tracing paper; clear tape; paintbrush; thin cardboard; glue stick; acrylic paints.

1. Make a hole with the craft knife at one end of the bottle. Push the scissors in and cut all around. Repeat at the other end.

2. Cut all the way up the tube in a straight line. Then wash the piece of plastic thoroughly and dry it well.

3. Trace the fish (see Templates opposite). Glue the trace onto the cardboard. Once the glue is dry, cut out the fish shape.

Curve

Place the fish like this.

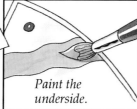

Paint the underside.

Overlap the tape a little.

4. Lay out the plastic with the curve as shown. Using the card shape, draw fish outlines on it with the waterproof pen.

5. Cut the fish out, just outside the pen line. Use bright paints to pattern them with scales, stripes and spots. Paint an eye.

6. Leave to dry, then paint in a background over the patterns. Both of these will show through on the other side.

7. When the paint is dry, cover the painted side with strips of clear tape. Neatly trim the tape all the way around the shape.

The straw goes on the taped side.

To string the fish, push fine elastic through the pieces of straw. Combine with other beads. You could make some rolled silver paper beads (see page 5).

8. Cut the straw into 1½cm (½in) lengths. Tape one piece across the back of each fish, 1½cm (½in) from the nose end.

Veined leaves

Follow steps 1-5 on the left, but use the leaf template. Instead of painting the back of the leaf, dab on a few blobs of paint.

Carefully press the side with paint on it against some plastic. Pull it off and leave it to dry.

Finish as for the fish, following steps 7-8, left.

You could string a plastic fish onto a leather thong with a bead on each side.

The background shades look nice if they mix together a little.

Seashell bracelet

You will need: a piece of plastic (made as in steps 1-2 opposite); waterproof felt-tip pen; ruler; clear tape; acrylic paints; paintbrush.

The strip must follow the curve.

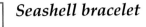

Paint right to the ends.

1. Use the ruler to draw a strip across the plastic. Make it long enough to pass over your hand, with a little to spare, and 3½cm (1½in) wide.

2. Cut the strip out. Paint shells and starfish on the inside of the curve. Leave to dry, then paint a background (see steps 5-6 opposite).

Fold the tape ends in and press down firmly.

3. Leave to dry, then back with tape (see step 7). To fasten, overlap the ends by ½cm (¼in). Put 7cm (3in) of tape where they join.

Templates

For the felt fish on page 19, trace the blue template.

For a leaf, trace this dark green shape.

Fish

Use this template to make flower beads like the ones at the top of the page.

Flower

Wire and gems

For a bracelet, you need: a bright foil chocolate wrapper; kitchen foil; old scissors; toothpick; about 45cm (18in) florists' wire (or fine brass or copper wire from a hardware store); a few small glass beads or about 15 small paper beads (see page 4).

1. Fold the wrapper around a little crumpled foil. Shape this so it is long and rounded. Press it flat on one side.

2. Straighten the wire by pulling it gently around a doorknob. Loop the middle around the foil shape as shown.

For coiling, see the box right.

For coiling, see the box right.

Coiling

Hold the wire tightly against a pencil. Wind the free end firmly five or six times around the pencil. Straighten the rest of it along the pencil. Slide the coil off. For a wavy effect, gently pull out the coil a little.

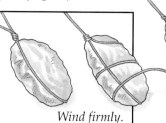

Wind firmly.

3. Gripping the wire together, twist the shape so the wire twists and joins. Wind one wire around the shape as shown.

4. Thread it through the middle wire at the other end of the shape and pull it through. This gem marks the middle of the bracelet.

5. Coil both wire ends, gently stretch the coils out and add a few glass beads. Finish with wire fastenings (see below).

Wire fastenings

You need: plastic straw; old scissors; blunt table knife; pliers. Once the wire bracelet is the right length, add 6cm (2½in) to each end and trim.

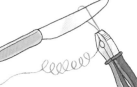

pliers. Twist the knife around a few times to join them. Slide the wire off the knife. Trim the loose end, then squeeze it in with the pliers.

Finish the hook by bending the shape over the straw and pressing it in a little.

The loop: make as shown on page 6, but use one toothpick.

For the hook: bend 4cm (1½in) of one end of the wire over the knife blade. Grip the wires with the

24

Gem necklace

What you need: rounded teaspoon of sea-salt crystals; food dye; household glue (PVA); toothpick; egg cup; plastic foodwrap; 150cm (5ft) florists' wire; a few paper beads (see page 6); tiny glass beads.

If you want to make a white gem, leave out the food dye.

This starts gelling at once.

1. Mix the salt and a drop of food dye in the egg cup. Add a teaspoon of glue and mix well.

2. As the mixture gels together, turn it onto the foodwrap. Push it into a rough pyramid shape.

3. Leave this gem to dry for 12 hours in a warm place. Paint on a coat of glue as varnish. Leave to dry.

4. Straighten the wire by pulling it gently around a doorknob, keeping the two ends together.

The back of the gem is its flattest side. The bottom is the pointed end.

5. Loop the middle around the gem. Twist the two wire ends together very tightly at the back.

Back

Front

A

6. Bend one wire down to the bottom. Wind it around and up two or three times to reach the top.

7. Twist the two wires together at the top. Push them both through a paper bead, then separate them.

8. Gently pull each wire into a curved, necklace shape between your thumb and fingers.

Finish with wire fastenings (see page 24).

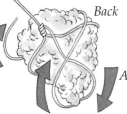

9. Thread beads onto each side, make coiled sections (see box) and thread with more beads.

25

Bright bracelets

These bracelets are made from left-over scraps of thin, pretty fabrics (old scarves or ties are also good). If you don't have any, buy small amounts of silky fabric, cotton or chiffon, plain or patterned. Mix different fabrics or use a single kind.

What you need: scraps of pretty fabrics; embroidery threads; felt; wadding or batting (padding from a fabric supplier); cardboard from a cereal box; scissors; ruler; pencil; needle; thread; pins; glue stick; clear tape; two paper clips.

1. Cut a 4cm (1½in) wide cardboard strip. Gently bend it into a curved shape.

The extra "tongue" is stuck down later on.

2cm (¾in)

2. Bend it in a circle that fits over your hand. Mark the end, add 2cm (¾in) and trim.

Outside of the bracelet (padded side)

3. Use this strip as a pattern to cut out a second strip. Glue them together.

Trim the padding to size.

Tongue

4. Trim the tongue's corners. Put glue on the strip and lay padding on it, up to the tongue.

Keep the padded side very neat.

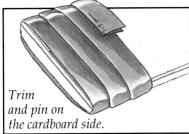

Trim and pin on the cardboard side.

5. Cut a strip of fabric 3 to 5cm wide (1¼-2in). Fold it neatly in half.

Attach with clear tape.

Start winding onto the cardboard side at the square end.

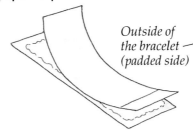

Folded edge

6. Wind the fabric strip around the cardboard a few times. Overlap the folded edges a little.

7. Trim the end of the fabric strip and pin it firmly to the fabric beneath it.

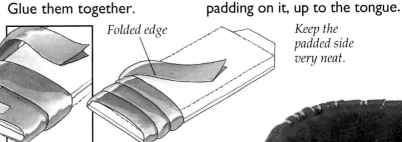

You can finish these bracelets in all kinds of ways. In step 10, you can pass the embroidery threads through tiny beads for added decoration. You can also tie off the threads on the cardboard side so that no ends show.

Try using small sections of metallic thread, which look wonderful.

If you want to use a plain fabric, try lining fabric. It is thin, silky and not expensive. It looks good on its own or mixed with patterned fabrics.

Add fabric up to the tongue.

8. Add more fabric strips in the same way, always starting with a 1cm (½in) overlap.

Tie off threads along an edge. Trim, leaving pretty ends.

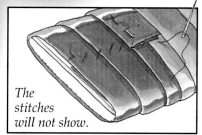

The stitches will not show.

9. Use big stitches to oversew along the middle of the unpadded side.

10. Remove the pins. Decorate by winding embroidery threads around in sections.

Sew neatly where the two ends join.

Tongue goes between the cardboard and the fabric.

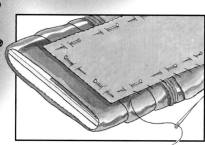

11. Pin a strip of felt to cover the stitches, then oversew and remove the pins.

12. Put glue on the top of the tongue, and slide it under the cardboard at the other end.

13. Hold the tongue with paper clips. Leave to dry, then sew the fabric edges together.

Glassy beads

What you need: plastic foodwrap; bright plastic straws; scissors; ruler. **Also:** scraps of a few things on this list: kitchen foil; tissue or crêpe paper; felt; bright foil chocolate wrappers; embroidery threads; tiny glass beads; foil Christmas decorations. For more ideas, see the photograph at the bottom of the opposite page.

For a rich, shimmery effect, wear two or three strands of glassy beads together.

You can mix glassy beads with washers and nuts (see box right), or with a few beads from a broken necklace.

Line the straw up with one side of the foodwrap.

1. Unroll 18cm (7in) of foodwrap. Lay a straw along the edge of the loose end.

2. Make a 13cm (5in) cut in the foodwrap where the straw ends.

Threading onto gift tie

Use silver or gold gift tie to make a glassy bead necklace. To make threading easier, tightly bind one end of the gift tie with tape.

For thick glassy beads, use fat straws and bind extra foodwrap around them. For fine beads, use thin straws.

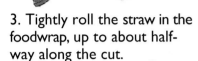

Leave a bare strip across the top.

3. Tightly roll the straw in the foodwrap, up to about half-way along the cut.

4. Scatter the scraps and threads so they criss-cross over the next 5cm (2in).

5. Continue binding the straw up firmly, tucking in the scraps and threads as you go.

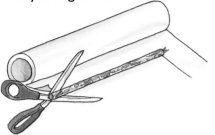

To seal in the scraps, roll and press gently all over.

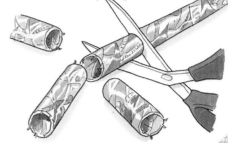

6. Carefully cut the bound straw away from the rest of the foodwrap.

7. Pressing gently, roll the straw on a flat surface under the palm of your hand.

8. Make beads by snipping into 2 or 3cm (¾in or 1in) lengths. Trim loose ends.

Here are things you can tuck into glassy beads. Cut fabric, paper and threads into tiny pieces.

Threading with washers

Try threading glassy beads with small metal washers from a hardware store. They are not expensive to buy, and they look good with other beads too.

Cup washers

Use brass washers (right) if there are gold scraps in the beads.

Try threading two cup washers back to back.

Embroidery threads

Different shades of felt and netting

Washers: try threading them in twos or threes between glassy beads.

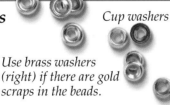

Also try small nuts like these, from a hardware store.

Sequins

Chocolate wrapper

Foil crêpe paper

Tiny glass beads

Silky bangles

For a silky bangle, you need: about 25cm (10in) plastic tubing from a pet shop (this is sold for use in fish tanks, and is not expensive at all); six-stranded embroidery silk; clear tape; craft knife; scissors; needle with a large eye.

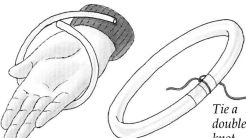

1. Cut a piece of tubing long enough to make a circle that can pass over your hand.

Tie a double knot.

2. Stick the two ends together with clear tape. Tie a thread to the right of this.

This bangle is made like a glitter bangle (see below right), but it is filled with tiny glass beads.

3. Trim the short end of the thread to 2cm (¾in), then tape it down as shown.

Push knot near the first knot.

4. Bring the long end around the tube, then pass it back through itself, making a knot.

5. Make lots of knots in this way. Keep them all lined up, neat and close together.

Use different shades to cover all the bangle.

6. Trim and tape the thread end. Now start with a new one, following steps 3-5.

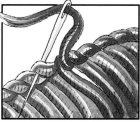

7. To finish, thread the free end on a needle. Sew it firmly into the first knot, then trim.

Here, metallic yarn is passed through a few clay beads (page 6) and glass ones for extra interest.

Seed bangle (fill a tube with seeds such as poppy and sesame).

For a very bright effect, use lots of different shades of thread.

Fringed bangle

You need: bangle made as in steps 1-2 on the left; knitting yarn; clear tape; craft knife; scissors; 8cm (3in) wide strip of cardboard.

Cut here. *8cm (3in)*

1. Wind some yarn six times around the cardboard. Cut at the bottom to make a six-stranded loop.

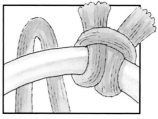

2. Place the loop as shown, take the ends around the bangle, up through the loop, then pull them tight.

3. Add fringed loops like this all the way around. To finish, trim all the fringes to the length you want.

Glitter bangles

If you like, you can hide the clear tape by binding some thread over it.

Glitter bangles

Stick a piece of clear tape over one end of a piece of plastic tubing. Pour some glitter into your hand, then scoop it into the tube until it is full.

Block the other end with tape, then tape the two ends together firmly.

For this bangle, fill a tube with tiny cake decorations.

Tape over the end.

31

Earrings and brooches

Here are some earring and brooch ideas based on earlier projects in this book.

For beads that have a loop, simply push an earring attachment through it.

Bead earrings

Use silvery florists' wire.

1. Cut a piece of wire as long as the bead. Bend it in half.

2. Put some household glue (PVA) into the top of the bead.

Use a toothpick to push the glue in.

Leave to dry.

3. Loop the wire through an earring attachment (page 3).

4. Gently push the two wire ends into the glued end of the bead.

Plant bead earrings (page 9)

Glassy bead earrings (page 28)

Paper earrings (page 4)

For a brooch like this, use paper beads (see page 4), or try rolled felt beads (page 18). Before gluing the beads on, paint the base or cover it with pretty paper.

Gem earrings: make gems (page 25), take their wires through beads, through attachments, and back the same way. Finish by twisting the wires around the back. Trim the ends.

Brooches

Glue beads onto a small piece of cardboard. Glue a brooch back (see page 3) onto the other side of this base.

This gem (page 25) is wrapped in wire, first tightly, then loosely with a few beads threaded on. Pass a safety pin through a few wires at the back to attach it.

Fabric brooches

Make a felt heart (page 18) and sew on an extra, small heart at the bottom. Sew a brooch back (see page 3) onto the back, or a safety pin, which is a good way to attach any type of fabric brooch.

The small heart is two layers of felt sewn together. Decorate by sewing on tiny glass beads.

First published in 1995 by Usborne Publishing Ltd, Usborne House, 83-85 Saffron Hill, London EC1N 8RT.
Copyright © 1995 Usborne Publishing Ltd.

Printed in Portugal. UE. First published in America in March 1996.